Table of Conte

This lesson plan book belongs to:

Name_____

School _____

Grade/Subject _____

Room_____

School Year _____

Address _____

Phone _____

Teacher Created Resources, Inc.
6421 Industry Way
Westminster, CA 92683
www.teachercreated.com
ISBN: 978-0-7439-3204-2
©2003 Teacher Created Resources, Inc.
Reprinted, 2008
Made in U.S.A.

Managing Editor: Karen Goldfluss, M.S. Ed.
Art Director: CJae Froshay
Cover Design: Barb Lorseyedi
Imaging: James Edward Grace
All Artwork ©Mary Engelbreit Inc.
www.maryengelbreit.com

Seating Chart (page 3)

A seating chart is provided for easy reference. Table and desk arrangements will vary throughout the year depending on room size, available furniture, grade level taught, teaching style, and academic program needs. To accommodate a variety of classroom arrangements, you may wish to create additional charts and place specific seating information in a separate folder.

Student Roster (pages 4 and 5)

Use the roster to record information for each student. Having the roster in your lesson plan book provides you with quick and easy access to important data for both you and a substitute teacher.

Birthdays (page 6)

Use the chart on this page to write students' names and birth dates. Recognize each special day with a birthday greeting. For young children, you may wish to sing to them.

Weekly Schedule (page 7)

If your schedule changes periodically, you may wish to duplicate this page before completing your current schedule. Attach new schedules throughout the year, as the need arises.

Year At A Glance (pages 8 and 9)

Use this chart to plan units of study and/or to focus on immediate and upcoming events, conferences, meetings, seminars, and other important dates. Record each event as soon as you are notified. The Year At A Glance chart can also be reproduced for students to help them plan projects and keep track of important dates and events.

Substitute Teacher Information (pages 10 and 11)

Document all pertinent information on these pages. If you have a copy of the layout of your school, attach it to page 11. Otherwise, sketch a diagram of the school building and grounds. Be sure to show important locations, such as the office, restrooms, faculty lounge, cafeteria, auditorium, and playground.

Any Time Activities (pages 12 and 13)

These activities can be used during transition periods when the teacher needs to help several students, to challenge students, or to provide students with meaningful work after they have completed required assignments. They are particularly handy for substitute teachers and may be initiated at "any time" of the day.

Indoor & Outdoor Games (pages 14 and 15)

The games listed on these pages suggest ways to involve students in organized activities during daily free-time periods or inclement weather. Early in the year, discuss rules of good conduct and sportsmanship with students. Keep a supply of board games, playing cards, and center activities that students can easily access. Decide how to choose teams fairly and have a system in place for rotating students among the games. For outdoor games, place equipment in a central location and give students the responsibility of distributing and returning all equipment.

Daily Lesson Plans (pages 16 – 95)

Use the Daily Lesson Plans section to help you organize your lesson plans each week. There are enough weekly plan pages to cover a 40-week school year. At the top of the left-hand page, fill in the blank to indicate the week dates for which the plans are written. The first column may be used for notes. For special programs requiring more in-depth explanation of plans, reference the specific folder, notebook, guide, etc., to which the teacher should be directed. This is especially helpful to substitute teachers.

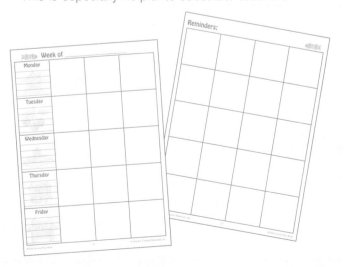

Seating Chart

Seat Arrangement Ideas

Sticky notes can be used to temporarily assign seats.

1. Basic Row Seating

2. U-Shaped Seating

3. Rectangle Seating

4. Partner Seating

The size and shape of your room will play a large part in your seating arrangement.

You may want to change this layout once you are familiar with your students and their needs.

Regardless of your seating plan, the most important concern is that you can easily see all your students and the children in turn have good visibility of you, the chalkboard, and other focal points in the room.

Front of Classroom

Student's Name	Parent's Name	Address
1.		
2.		
3.		
4.		
5.		
6.		
7.		
8.		
9.		
10.		
11.		
12.		
13.		
14.		
15.		
16.		
17.		
18.		
19.		
20.		
21.		
22.		
23.		
24.		
25.		
26.		
27.		
28.		
29.		
30.		
31.		
32.		
33.		
34.		
35.		
36.		

Roster

Home & Work Phones	Birthday	Siblings	Notes

Birthdays

August	September	October
November	**December**	**January**
February	**March**	**April**
May	**June**	**July**

Weekly Schedule

Time	Monday	Tuesday	Wednesday	Thursday	Friday

SEPTEMBER

OCTOBER

JANUARY

FEBRUARY

MAY

JUNE

A Glance

NOVEMBER

DECEMBER

MARCH

APRIL

JULY

AUGUST

Substitute Teacher

School Schedule

- Class Begins_____
- Morning Recess_____
- Lunchtime _____
- Class Resumes_____
- Afternoon Recess_____
- Dismissal _____

Special Notes

_____
_____
_____
_____
_____
_____
_____
_____
_____

Special Classes

Student _____

Class _____ Day _____ Time _____

Student _____

Class _____ Day _____ Time _____

Student _____

Class _____ Day _____ Time _____

Special Needs Students

Where to Find

- Class List _____
- School Layout_____
- Seating Chart _____
- Attendance Record_____
- Lesson Plans _____
- Teacher Manuals_____
- First Aid Kit_____
- Emergency Information _____
- Supplementary Activities _____
- Class Supplies–paper, pencils, etc._____
- Referral forms and procedures_____

_____
_____
_____
_____
_____
_____
_____
_____
_____
_____

Student	Needs	Time and Place

Information

Classroom Standards

- When finished with an assignment

  _____

  _____

- When and how to speak out in class

  _____

  _____

- Incentive Program

  _____

  _____

- Discipline

  _____

  _____

- Restroom Procedure

  _____

  _____

People Who Can Help

- Teacher/Room _____

- Dependable Students _____

  _____

  _____

  _____

  _____

  _____

- Principal _____

- Secretary _____

- Custodian _____

- Counselor _____

- Nurse _____

Layout of School

1. Play 5 x 5. This is easily accomplished by making a grid of 25 squares. Choose five categories. Place one on the top of each box. Then randomly choose five letters and place one in each box down the side. Have students call out words that fit each category. This is really handy when working with a theme that you wish to review.

2. Use the game of Charades to reinforce and review material. Choose spelling or vocabulary words, titles of books by authors the class has studied, or activities going on in school. Put these on slips of paper and place in a container. Let individuals or groups of students choose one and act it out.

3. Read aloud to your class! Keep some funny, short stories or a book of limericks available for a quick read.

4. Play "baseball." Choose a skill that needs to be reviewed. Draw a baseball diamond on the board. Choose a scorekeeper. Divide the class into two teams. Determine which team is up first. Ask each player a review question. If the player answers correctly, have him or her run the bases by marking the base on the diamond on the board. A run is scored every time a player touches home base. If the team misses three questions, the other team is up.

5. Try some rhythms. Clap or tap out a rhythm and then have students repeat it. Vary the patterns and the lengths, making them increasingly more challenging.

6. Choose a category such as food, movies, or places, and challenge students to think of one for each letter of the alphabet.

7. Select a category such as famous people. Have one student say the name. The next student must name another famous person whose first name begins with the last letter of the person's name (for example, George Bush, Harriet Tubman, Nancy Reagan).

8. Ask students a number of questions such as: Is there anyone whose phone number digits add up to 30? or Whose birthday is closest to the date when man first walked on the moon (or any other date you have been studying)? or If you add the ages of everyone in your family, who has the highest number? Who has the lowest?

9. Create a spelling chain. All students stand. Give them a spelling word. The first person says the first letter, the second gives the second letter, and so on. If a student gives the wrong letter, he/she must sit down.

10. Play "guess the characteristic." Ask several students who all have something in common to stand. The class, including the standing students, must guess what they all have in common, such as they all have shoes with no laces, they all walk to school, or they are all in band.

11. Do a daily edit to start the day or fill small spaces of time. These become writing skill mini-lessons. Lift an incorrect sentence directly from students' writing or create one that include errors students are commonly making. You may wish to focus on one skill at a time. Print the incorrect sentence(s) on the board or overhead. Have students edit the sentence and write it correctly in a section of their journals or a special notebook that can be used for reference. Follow up at some time during the day with a class discussion so the students can finalize their corrections and see that there may be more than one way to solve a writing problem.

Activities

12. An especially effective daily edit that promotes more interesting writing is Expand-a-Sentence. Give students a very simple sentence (e.g., The child ran.) Include insert marks where you want students to add words and underline words that they may change to something more exciting. Model an expansion for students the first time you do this activity. The new sentence may become: The very excited young lady raced wildly down the street with her red braids swirling around in the air.

13. Keep a supply of board and table games that require strategy and logical thinking. Use them for special fill-in times like rainy day recesses. Good examples of commercial games are Scrabble, Monopoly, Boggle, and Chutes and Ladders.

14. Collect word searches, crossword puzzles, and kids' pages from Sunday comics. Laminate them for wipe-off reuse.

15. Save about-to-be discarded paper with at least one blank side (computer printouts, old dittos, faded construction paper, etc.). Use the paper for free-drawing time. Also encourage students to free-write; many of them also improve creativity and expertise in drawing with practice.

16. Derive many words from one. Copy on the blackboard a multi-syllabic word taken from a theme or topic of the day. Ask students to write as many words from this as they can in a specified time. Only letters from the original word may be used. This activity can be done in small groups or individually.

17. Set up a magnetic board center for sponge activities. Divide the board into "yes" and "no" columns. Prepare a magnetic name tag for each student by gluing a tagboard square with the student's name onto a piece of magnetic strip (available at fabric or sign stores). On the board, pose daily questions which involve critical thinking, opinions, or problem-solving activities. The questions must have either a yes or no answer. Have students place their magnetic name tags in the appropriate column. Discuss responses.

18. Read a short story, poem, essay, news articles, etc., to the class. Have students write a short first impression of it. Compare student responses.

19. Play "Three-in-a-Row." Make game boards from 8 ½" x 11" (22 cm x 28 cm) pieces of tagboard, cardboard, or index paper. Divide each game board into nine equal boxes. Provide X and O cards (five of each) for each game board. (Be sure the cards fit into the boxes.)

    Two students use one game board; one using X cards and the other using O cards. Use this game for reinforcement or review. When a student responds correctly to a problem or activity, he/she places a card in a box. If incorrect, the player loses a turn. The first player to achieve three in a row vertically, horizontally, or diagonally is the winner.

20. Incorporate a "Brainteaser Time" into your day. Choose from a selection of brainteaser activities or have students make up some of their own. These can be presented to the class as part of your daily sponge activities.

Indoor Games

Silent Ball

Equipment: soft foam ball or sponge

To play: This game is a quiet classic. Begin with all students seated on their desks. A soft sponge or foam ball is tossed from one student to another with no talking allowed. Players who drop the ball, throw too hard, or talk must sit in their seats. Continue play until only one student is sitting on his or her desk.

I'm Going to New York

This is a game of listening and memory skills. The object of the game is to make a long, alphabetical list of items the students will take with them on a trip to New York, each student adding an item in alphabetical order from A to Z and then repeating all the items named before his or her turn. So, by the time play reaches student number four, he or she will say, "I am going to New York, and I am going to take a dog, a cup, a ball, and an apple." Play continues through the alphabet and around the circle. When a child cannot remember what comes next, he or she drops out of the circle and play continues from that point. Make this game relevant with variations, such as, "I'm going on safari," with students listing animals, or "I'm going to the American Revolution," with students listing historic figures and events.

Inside Baseball

This game is great for reviewing a variety of subjects. Decide where each "base" will be in your class. (It is more fun to play if the children get to move around.) Divide the class into two teams. You may want to let each team choose its name and write that on the chalkboard with "runs" and "outs" listed under it. As the first batter comes up, he or she may ask for a single, double, triple, or home run to designate the difficulty of the question he or she would like to answer. Take into account the student's ability when you "throw" a question at him or her. If the child gets a "hit," then he or she gets to go to the corresponding base. If, on the other hand, the child gets an "out," his or her play is ended until it is his or her turn again, and you can use the question with the next player who asks for the same level of difficulty.

Spell It Backwards

Students need to concentrate for this game. Players sit on their desks. Give the first player a simple word to spell. He or she spells one letter of the word going backwards and then the next in line gives the next-to-last letter, etc. If a mistake is made, that player sits down or gets a point against him, and the play continues.

20 Questions

This game is good for subject review. A student thinks of an item. Students then ask questions that can be answered "yes" or "no." The student who guesses the item then chooses the next item to be guessed. It takes a bit of practice to get the hang of this game, but it is well worth it for many subject areas.

Outdoor Games

Steal the Bacon

Equipment: an object such as a chalkboard eraser to use as the "bacon"

To play: Divide the class into two teams and place them into two lines facing each other. Assign each player a number. (If there is an extra player, then the last player on the other team gets two numbers.) Place the "bacon" between the lines. The teacher calls a number and the two players having that number race for the bacon. The bacon must not be hit or kicked out of position, but grabbed and run with all the way across the team's line. A point is scored if a player is tagged by the other player whose number was called or if the player can make it back to his own side. Be sure to keep track of the numbers you've already called with a pencil and paper.

Streets and Alleys

Equipment: no equipment needed for this game

To play: Choose three students: caller, cat, and mouse. The remaining students line up in neat rows and columns, their arms raised and touching. The caller faces away from the class. Starting at the opposite corners, the cat runs through the rows trying to catch the mouse without cutting through any line of students. At any time, the caller may shout, "Change!" and the class changes from rows to columns, or vice versa. Play until the mouse is caught; the players then choose someone new to take their places.

"Horse" Basketball

Equipment: basketball and court for each team—team size may vary

To play: Divide the class into as many groups as you have hoops. The first person on a team makes a shot, any shot. If the player misses, then he or she moves to the end of the line and it's the next person's turn. If a basket is made, then the person behind that shooter must make the same type of shot. If the second player makes the shot, then it's the next person's turn. The first person who misses a shot gets the letter H—on the way to spelling "Horse." The player who comes after a missed shot may make any type of shot. When the entire word "Horse" is spelled by any player, then that player is out. Play continues until there is only one player left. "Horse" also can be changed to "Rat" or "Elephant," etc., depending on the time and skill involved.

Kickball-Basketball

Equipment: a basketball court surrounded by lots of room and a kickball or soccer ball

To play: The object of this game is for the outfield team to make a basket before the player who is up runs around the edge of the basketball court to "home." Divide the class into two teams. Line one team up at the corner of the court, which becomes home plate. Play is like regular kickball, except the kicker runs all around the edges of the basketball court to score. The runner is out only when the outfield team brings the ball back to the court and makes a basket before the runner makes it around the court. Less-skilled players can drop kick the ball; use two courts to run around if your class is just learning to shoot.

 # Week of _____

Monday			
Tuesday			
Wednesday			
Thursday			
Friday			

Reminders:

 # Week of _____

Monday			
Tuesday			
Wednesday			
Thursday			
Friday			

Reminders:

Week of _____

Monday			
Tuesday			
Wednesday			
Thursday			
Friday			

Reminders:

 # Week of _____

Monday			

Tuesday			

Wednesday			

Thursday			

Friday			

Reminders:

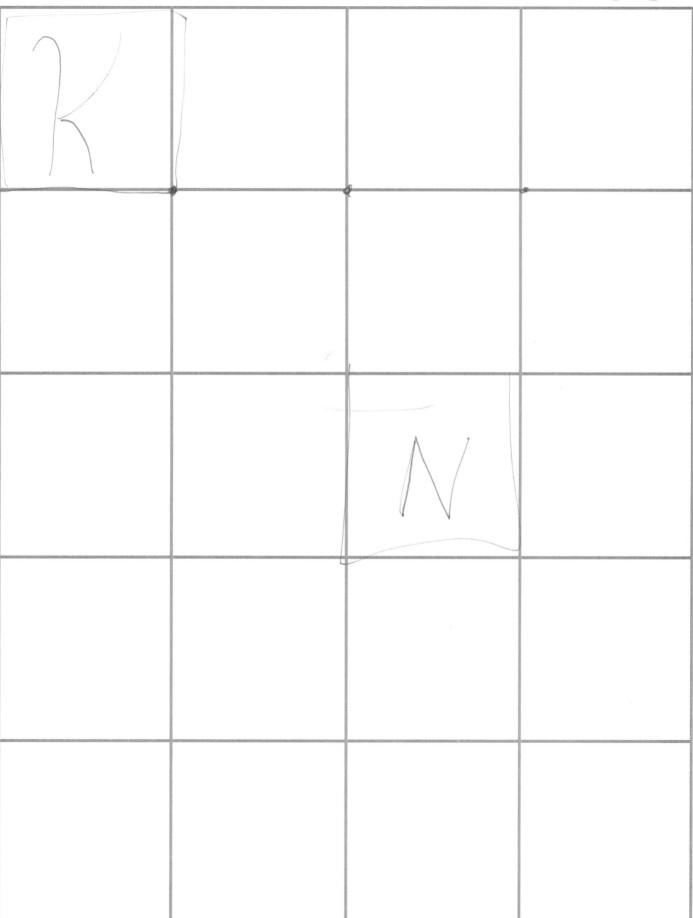

 Week of _____

Monday			
Tuesday			
Wednesday			
Thursday			
Friday			

Reminders:

Week of _____

Monday			
Tuesday			
Wednesday			
Thursday			
Friday			

Reminders:

Week of _____

Monday			
Tuesday			
Wednesday			
Thursday			
Friday			

Reminders:

Week of _____

Monday			

Tuesday			

Wednesday			

Thursday			

Friday			

Reminders:

Week of _____

Monday			
Tuesday			
Wednesday			
Thursday			
Friday			

Reminders:

Week of _____

Monday			
Tuesday			
Wednesday			
Thursday			
Friday			

Reminders:

Week of _____

Monday			
Tuesday			
Wednesday			
Thursday			
Friday			

Reminders:

Week of _____

Monday			
Tuesday			
Wednesday			
Thursday			
Friday			

Reminders:

Week of _____

Monday			
Tuesday			
Wednesday			
Thursday			
Friday			

Reminders:

Week of _____

Monday			
Tuesday			
Wednesday			
Thursday			
Friday			

Reminders:

Week of _____

Monday			

Tuesday			

Wednesday			

Thursday			

Friday			

Reminders:

Week of _____

Monday			

Tuesday			

Wednesday			

Thursday			

Friday			

Reminders:

Week of _____

Monday			
Tuesday			
Wednesday			
Thursday			
Friday			

Reminders:

Week of _____

Monday			
Tuesday			
Wednesday			
Thursday			
Friday			

Reminders:

Week of _____

Monday			

Tuesday			

Wednesday			

Thursday			

Friday			

Reminders:

Week of _____

Monday			
Tuesday			
Wednesday			
Thursday			
Friday			

Reminders:

Week of _____

Monday			

Tuesday			

Wednesday			

Thursday			

Friday			

Reminders:

Week of _____

Monday			

Tuesday			

Wednesday			

Thursday			

Friday			

Reminders:

Week of _____

Monday			
Tuesday			
Wednesday			
Thursday			
Friday			

Reminders:

 # Week of _____

Monday			
Tuesday			
Wednesday			
Thursday			
Friday			

Reminders:

Week of _____

Monday			
Tuesday			
Wednesday			
Thursday			
Friday			

Reminders:

Week of _____

Monday			
Tuesday			
Wednesday			
Thursday			
Friday			

Reminders:

Week of _____

Monday			
Tuesday			
Wednesday			
Thursday			
Friday			

Reminders:

Week of _____

Monday			

Tuesday			

Wednesday			

Thursday			

Friday			

Reminders:

Week of _____

Monday			
Tuesday			
Wednesday			
Thursday			
Friday			

Reminders:

Week of _____

Monday			
Tuesday			
Wednesday			
Thursday			
Friday			

Reminders:

Week of _____

Monday			
Tuesday			
Wednesday			
Thursday			
Friday			

Reminders:

Week of _____

Monday			

Tuesday			

Wednesday			

Thursday			

Friday			

Reminders:

Week of _____

Monday			

Tuesday			

Wednesday			

Thursday			

Friday			

Reminders:

Week of _____

Monday			
Tuesday			
Wednesday			
Thursday			
Friday			

Reminders:

 Week of _____

Monday			
Tuesday			
Wednesday			
Thursday			
Friday			

Reminders:

Week of _____

Monday			
Tuesday			
Wednesday			
Thursday			
Friday			

Reminders:

Week of _____

Monday			

Tuesday			

Wednesday			

Thursday			

Friday			

Reminders:

Week of _____

Monday			
Tuesday			
Wednesday			
Thursday			
Friday			

Reminders:

Week of _____

Monday			
Tuesday			
Wednesday			
Thursday			
Friday			

Reminders:

Notes

96